unremarkable girl's lullaby

to the moon, those who lay awake underneath it, and Alex Trebek

a mother sits, fast asleep, beside her baby,

as the little thing coos softly, the embers of stars trapped
in her eyes

and in her infant ears, she hears the voice of another, from
Elsewhere:

a voice that embodies all that is ardent and otherworldly—

a voice that makes a home past the marrow of the new
one's bones,

past the air in her lungs,

past the nervous wreck of her mortality,

and into the part of her that is timeless—

the part of her that will exist long after the world forgets
her body ever did.

every word the voice murmurs sounds like a promise,

and in a tone as elusive as a cloud, it whispers,

"you are not a work of art—

you are the synchronous exhalation of thousands of
celestial bodies

a masterpiece of reincarnating bits of energy, and stray morsels of tenderness

you are a heap of every human emotion:

of booming rage and beaming joy,

of blubbering grief and blushing affection,

of the echo of a scream that caresses the corners of the corner-less universe—

the culmination of everything and nothing, all at once—

so full of stagnation, and so full of chaos,

that there is nothing more for you to do on this earthly plane

than *supernova*—

and what a sight you will be

what a sight you will be."

this is the lullaby an unremarkable girl wrote

after a sleepless, starless night of her own

eleven twelve

if eleven ten brings contemplation,

and eleven eleven a plea,

then eleven twelve is the self-reflection

that comes to sit with me

snap out of it! you are not a *soul*,

you are a network of cells—

a lumpy pile of misfiring synapses

that send love letters to one another

through the perceived fissures between neurons

you are something new, made out of something borrowed;

a promise for an almost-brighter future,

and a relic of what has passed

you are the *dayhourminutesecond* you took your first breath,

the heralding cry that came with it,

and *nothing more*—

all wrapped up into one, unassuming,

unremarkable body

- welcome back to reality

we are not the names we were given at birth

by the time we waste away—

perhaps we never were in the first place;

perhaps we were never meant to be

                          - we are not our names

"are you excited

to be more than just somebody,

someday?"

"well, who will i be?"

"you will be all i am, and more.

you will be what i know lies within you…

and what i wish i could be."

"and will you be happy?"

"not happy, no; never happy—

but i will be absolved,

and i will be free."

"and me?

what will i be?"

what will i be?

- what will i be?

my younger self asks to be modeled after happy endings—

after the velvet tranquility of clear, cloudless skies

after the neon lights of city nights

after the sweetness of a plump blueberry's purple juice as it runs down the length of greedy fingers—

so i model her after the pale green-blue of the polluted water

that burbles under tall bridges

- close enough

the fortune cookie tells me that "april showers bring may flowers,"

but my calendar claims tomorrow's february, not april,

and i haven't seen a flower in forever

- it hasn't stopped raining

i feel as though i'm just pretty.

no, there's nothing wrong with me;

i am simply no mysterious Cleopatra,

no delicate Marie

really, i feel as though i'm just pretty—

and no, there's nothing wrong with me.

i am no Cassiopeia at her mirror,

no enchanting Hecate—

no, i feel as though i'm just pretty,

and there's nothing wrong with me.

- definably pretty

"it sounds like you hate your life a little."

"well, i think you all do, too—

since the compulsion lurks in between the wails of toddlers in their terrible twos,

and before the excitement that comes with surprise bouquets

i think it likes to trick us by ringing our doorbells at night with its invisible fingers,

and when we open our homes up to thin, still air,

the hate creeps in.

the hate creeps in."

                              - the hate creeps in

i can't wait for the day the moon decides to be selfish,

and saves some twinkle for herself

- she deserves better

there are bits of yellow in blue sadness—

the forced smile that battles threatening tears for dominance

there are bits of blue in yellow contentment—

the bright eyes that look back on aging, fading memories

- look harder

i like to sing until my throat's on fire/and i like to dance until my shoes are worn to their soles/i like to write until my hand hangs from my wrist/like a ripe mango from its arching branch/and i like to read until my eyes short-circuit/and force shutdown/i like to sit and listen to the merry jingles of ice cream trucks/and to the white noise of sunshine/to the genial hum of the earth/and to the silent, lingering threat of its prophesied extinction/i like to breathe all of the outside in/and i like to *live*/i like to live

- i like to live

aren't we such artless beings

to believe that love can save us?

to put faith into candied words,

and to grow to loathe cold, lonesome nights?

- wide-eyed fools

i slipped on my old prom dress,

and yearned for it to be the gown i would one day be buried
in—

immortalized in the night

that i promised myself nothing would change

- things have changed

what's the point in taking love seriously

when no one else does?

i'm bored of the *nothingness* that lingers after kisses, the polite smiles casual lovers wear like masks

no, i want consumption;

i want something i'd kill for—

i want to implode with the heat of a thousand hearts

- where's the love i daydreamed about?

there are kisses/and then, there are *kisses*/the ones that shimmer and die like the tail-ends of fireworks/and then, the ones that *are* the fireworks/the ones that are like the red and blue lights of ambulances approaching car crashes(/the response to the destruction)/and then, the ones that *are* the car crash(/the destruction itself)/there are kisses/and then, there are *kisses*/the ones that kill you a little on the inside/and then, the ones that are the cause of your *rebirth*/there are kisses/and then/there are *kisses*

- there are kisses/and then, there are kisses

and here comes the breath

the stillness

the *afterglow*—

the moment when two bits of stardust

realize they've met before

                                        - afterglow

i like the steadiness of your breath as you dream/and i like the sigh that means you've startled yourself awake/i like the warmth you exude as you giggle your way through kisses/and i like the sweet smile that smites my thoughts as you pull away/i like your light/and i like your dark/the pleasure of your good humor bestowed upon me/and the barrenness of your bad days that i suffer through, too/i like who you are/and i don't care about who you aren't/because i like to love *you*/i like to love you

- i like to love you

i think you sing about me in the shower

- and i hope the neighbors hear

please don't kiss my skin unless you intend to stay.

it'll remember the impression of your lips

like the relief an EpiPen brings after an allergic reaction

the second you stop touching me,

my skin'll flare up again—

an infinite cycle of discomfort,

and disappointment.

so please don't kiss my skin unless you intend to stay

because i'd rather teach the organ to forget you,

than go into anaphylactic shock

- i've had it up to here with allergies

i hadn't lived before i met you,

but god, at least it was freer than this

- free as a bird in a cage with a door

i told you that i'd wait for you until my hair went grey

until i couldn't see past my hands

until i couldn't get out of bed in the morning

until all i could remember

was the sound of your voice—

and you smiled in your secret way,

and told me you loved me, too

- how was i supposed to know that that *was what love meant?*

in my head now sleeps

a darling little golden boy

he is made of our shared laughter,

and the blue, winter sunlight that peeks

through the window blinds,

and wakes

the space between my eyes

he is made of the melted chocolate chips that sit atop
homemade cookies,

and cold feet.

He kissed me like I was his lover in another lifetime,

and gossips about me with my reflection

- darling little golden boy

and i'm afraid he loves me in phases of the moon

in the emptiness of New,

and in the consumption of Full

in the will they/won't they of Waxing,

and in the inevitable end of Waning

it is not intrinsic,

but conditional—

not evasive, like sunlight,

but aloof, like starshine—

and something that only exists

in the quiet of night

- he loves me in phases of the moon

i read your diary while you were asleep,

and found no mention of me but one:

"on thursday, i kissed the girl with sadness in her eyes,

and now the same girl

is warming my bed.

oh, what a monster i am—

what a monster i've become."

- invasion of privacy

a recycling bin sits in the corner of your room

into which you dispose of the emotions

that are too complicated for you to decipher

the night you threw the love you felt for me away,

i praised you,

because at least you chose to save the planet

as opposed to littering it

with the radioactive waste

that no one else wants.

- save the planet!

i let you harvest the ripe fruit of my heart

until my chest was a barren field

       - and it was just *starting to bear crop again*

his heart has a body count,

and it is an unimpressively long list—

filled with pages of names of people, foreign to me,

who must love the same way i do

- his heart has a body count

i must have walked under one-too-many ladders

to have been cursed with knowing you

                                        - jinx!

i've been burning the memories i have left of you to
ash/and the remnants of your kisses actually make for
good kindling/they'd been baking me from the inside-out
anyways/after being ignited by the sheer heat that once
radiated from my heart/so i decided i might as well put
them to better use

- kisses as kindling

summer is the season that kills itself and makes you watch
its decomposition:

the time of the year you'll try to peel from your skin like
the scab of a sunburn,

or a person

- variations on one of the four seasons

i'm a bit stuck in the end credits of our movie—

lips retaining the heat from the weight of our first and final kiss,

and a star or two in my half-closed eyes

- colloquial

some things are just coincidences—

and some people

                                        - it's as easy as that

i've forgotten what color your eyes are,

because i've allowed myself to become enraptured with the stars in my own

i've forgotten just how much pleasure i took from waking up beside you,

because i've spent hours lecturing my body on the pros of having a bed to itself

i've forgotten what it is to consider my heart a jigsaw puzzle,

because i've come to the realization that *i am not incomplete* without the missing piece that i thought was yours

i've forgotten what it is to love you,

and yet—

and yet

and yet

- i never learn, do i?

on my way back to you, i took note of where you looked
for me,

since you left behind pieces of yourself like breadcrumbs
leading out of a forest

your keys were on our table at the café,

and your glasses were on my nightstand

how'd you lose your shoelaces in the pond,

and your jacket on the bench at the park?

you've always been so forgetful,

(and i've always loved you, all the same)

so i've been picking your pieces up,

hoarding them like a squirrel does with his acorns,

and i'll offer them to you, along with a kiss,

when i see you again

- omw

all this love, but still:

life is not a movie

                              - even though i wish it was

one twenty-three

i tripped and fell into a black hole of obsession/and as the
light was stolen from my eyes/the bottomless chasm
asked after your middle name/your favorite color/your
home address

first, let your body settle against your bed/like it's your casket, and you're headed six feet under/only, unlike the dead, no rest will come/just the grey ghost of your last apathetic lover/who's waited all day long/to haunt your sleepless dreams

- the insomniac's guide to lucid dreaming

"are you mad at yourself?"

my reflection asks me one night as she paints my nails,

and bluntly,

i answer, "yes,"

because i'm sick of telling lies

"and i'm not sure it'll ever end.

it comes during the moments

that are riddled with inadequacy;

in razor-sharp contemplations at the height of night

in smooth shots of gasoline.

it comes as i frantically twirl pencils between my fingers
like batons,

and when i tap my toes against linoleum,

anticipating fantasized moments that will never be

it comes when i soothe myself to sleep,

and it comes when i sigh myself awake

it comes when i can't breathe,

and when it comes,

i breathe again."

    - another therapy session with my reflection

in everything she does, she expresses,

and what a marvel she is to behold

as she writes dissertations into the margins of borrowed
books,

and falls asleep to the sound of *whatever'sontv*

in everything she does, she expresses,

and what a marvel she is to behold

as she sits, her feet dangling, off the edge of a cliff,

screaming bloody murder

into its gaping, unexplored abyss

- in everything she does, she expresses

i am no raw diamond to be refined/i am not even the shiny side of a gum wrapper/i am the bits of worthless rock/that scatter about the ground once you break me open/i am the thoroughly chewed, spit-out gum/now flavorless

- i am no diamond

my heart is made of intricate clockwork,

and the tired odds and ends

of this ticking time machine

have been *waitingwaitingwaiting*

for love to come their way

- this clockwork heart of mine

     unremarkable girl's lullaby

i hold hands with leeches

with parasites

with incubi in skin suits

who sap the love out of me until

i am nothing but blushless

- on the topic of making dire mistakes

"ow," says your body,

but you tell it to hush, teeth grit in concentration

there's nothing to be afraid of

"there's nothing to be afraid of."

there's nothing to be afraid of

"ow," says your body,

but this time, it hushes itself

there's nothing to be afraid of

"there's nothing to be afraid of."

there's *nothing*

(be afraid)

- there's nothing to be afraid of

i shouldn't be allowed to fall in love/i always take the wrong turn/i don't stir enough/i put weeds into vases and call them lilacs/i willfully ignore/what's between the lines

- in short, i'm an idiot

beside her, he sleeps,

her innocence smeared across his skin like body paint,

and his chest rising and falling with the ease of a young child

it's almost as if

he hasn't just killed someone,

but really, how is he to know what he's done?

after all, it's not like there's any blood—

just red, parallel scratches,

an aching scalp,

and eyes that cry for resuscitation

so instead of condemning him,

she turns on her side and looks out the window,

and with a gasp, realizes that the night is *beautiful*:

an inky blanket, littered with the sharp brilliance of white stars

that she wishes to walk into

so that she may be, for once,

(consensually) consumed

- to be consumed

i plant seeds of myself into everything i touch—

into tea saucers and hair ties and bed clothes and picture
frames

into doorknobs and acetone and plastic cacti and winter
coats

into chipping wallpaper and unmade beds and mystery
stains and drooping forget-me-nots—

so that even the most mundane objects, once sprouted,

remind past lovers, strikingly, of me

- memories: my favorite kind of budding flower

   unremarkable girl's lullaby

you knew just the right strings/muscles

to pluck/pull

to make the violin/my body

screech

- screech

"oh," breathes your body,

and there is something *being born* within the exhalation:

the beginnings of something new,

and precious,

and trusting—

accompanied with the ardent hope that it stays that way

"oh," breathes your body,

and you'd be a hypocrite to tell it to hush

there's something to be afraid of

there's something to be afraid of

there's *something*

(be afraid)

                                        *- there's *something to be afraid of*

in this body made of colors/with pink lips that can turn blue/i become a prism of light when you touch me/casting rainbows all over you

- in this body made of colors

one told her he loved her,

and she didn't feel a thing

another told her she was something special,

      and she felt everything at once

- divine timing/divine people

i have kisses buried into my palms

they do not burn, they do not ache,

and still, i wish i could scratch at them,

draw them out like blood samples,

cut my hands to stumps and be done with the whole mess—

rather than have to remember

who put the kisses there in the first place

- buried kisses

we had that nervous kind of love—

the type that hides behind its mother's leg,

and scarcely says a word

- skinny

i saw my heart in your trash can today/veins bulging as it beat with pained effort/"poor thing," i murmured/as my hands went to cup it/"poor thing," i murmured/as it labored weakly in my grasp/"poor thing," i murmured/as i shoved it/dirt and all/back into my chest

- poor thing

when i think of you, it snows

and not just a polite, little sprinkle,

but a violent ice storm of pent-up emotion

that seems to be just as sick and tired of missing you

as i am growing to be

- let it snow

the burden of wasted love weighs heavily on her spine,

and aches like an old war wound

whenever apparitions of love songs

permeate the cavity in her chest

- wasted love

you didn't need an iron to brand me—

the fire in your eyes was ample enough

- that being said, look somewhere else

i've met my fair share of serial killers,

but none as daring as you—

you, who showed me your treasure trove of blood-drained
hearts,

with the same hands that left bright red prints around my
throat

i've met my fair share of serial killers,

but none as daring as you—

you, who smiled as you leaned in to kiss me,

and told me that i'd be next

- plot twist!

i am unsure of what i want/so my mind gives me everything at once/it gives me high-pitched peals of laughter/and it drowns me in bouts of bitter tears/it gives me the breath of relief that comes after the sadness/the emptiness/and the rage/take a collective step off my chest/and then it makes me hold said breath/so that my lungs and i know to be grateful/it gives me cravings for vanilla ice cream/and it walks me into liquor stores/it gives me memories of you/and memories that chronicle me, being just fine on my own/it gives me time to rest/and it makes me soldier on/it lets my curious fingers reach out and touch egyptian cotton/and it stops anything/that tries to reach out and touch me

- i'm the very definition of caprice

beware of monsters with kind eyes

and cherub cheeks

that touch you when you want them to

(but not why)

- beware!

one comes to the other, in pieces/and asks to be remade/"i only have extra pieces of me," the other argues/"i swear, you are more than enough"/the other looks for the one, in pieces/hoping to ask for the return of their spares/but no matter how hard they search for them/the other can't find the one/the other/can't find/the one

- the other/can't find/the one

i keep wasting wishes on you,

and as much as i want to blame you for it,

it's me who's been pummeling my better judgement to a
bleeding pulp

before trying to will you beside me

i keep wasting wishes on you,

and it's easier to pretend that i hate you endlessly for it

more than i hate myself

for wanting them to *just come true already*

- i'm supposed to know better

he told me i reminded him of my mother, the moon,

and it didn't sound like a compliment, so i said, "oh? well, why?"

"you see, the sun shines on every ugly part of us—our faces, our faults, our fears—whether we want it to or not," he said,

"but the moon? she asks for nothing,

and expects nothing.

she shoos away the sun, then drenches the sky in onyx,

and dotes on us

as we fall asleep."

offended for artemis, i asked him why he sounded disappointed,

but he only shook his head

"i guess this is my way of asking if anyone looks after you," he said,

"since no one looks after the moon."

- who looks after the moon?

love is not an escape,

you tired, bloodless thing

love is the plea in prayers that go unanswered,

and love is the smothering solitude of tables-for-one

love is all fall and no destination,

and love is a purgatory

for those unlucky enough to trip

- the in-between

wilting flowers bend to me as i walk by,

and i wish there was something more for them that i could do,

the same way pieces of my heart litter the floor like the ripped-out pages of my ship-wrecked emotions,

and i wish there was something more for me that i could do

- i wish there was something more i could do

i am the five-point star that sits atop your christmas tree,

skin aglow with passionate praise and gold paint that
glitters

you gaze up at me with the eyes of a blind worshipper—

what good have i done to get to be up here?

i am the confetti—with champagne for adhesive—

that clings to the naked stretches of your skin on new
years' eve

i watch you slumber with the mauve desire for something
that's just out of reach (you're too far away when you're
asleep),

and let the thumb that's closest to your face trail across
your lips at 12:02 (they're still red from kissing me)

i am the white roses that make up your wife's bouquet on
your wedding day

my real body didn't get an invitation, as expected,

but apparently, neither did your proclaimed love for
her—

i can hear the silence that sobs its way out of your eyes

as you lie to yourself for the millionth time,

and whisper, "i do."

- roses can't object

there exists, lost in space, an astronaut boy

he thought he would be dead by now,

but instead, he floats, keeping vigil over the world,

blue-lipped and fingers gloved, yet frostbitten

from his star's-eye view, he watches the tumbling ocean
waves with feigned interest,

as well as the airplanes that soar through the sky, partially
hidden by water vapor,

and the people who spend their time climbing to the tops
of seemingly unconquerable mountains

but his end is coming—he knows it

and even as his vision starts to wane,

he muscles down his panic, as it is futile,

and asks the universe for one final sight—

not for the ocean waves, the airplanes, or the people on the
peaks of mountains, mind you—

but for one, unremarkable girl,

who has been waiting to see the astronaut boy again

since he first took off

in his godforsaken rocket

    - the astronaut boy, and our unremarkable girl

i look at myself in the mirror and say, "you're allowed to be the plants that grow in december,

and you're allowed to be the rainfall that strikes on days once plagued by blue skies

"you're allowed to be the anticipation that comes hand-in-hand with the flip of a coin,

and you're allowed to be a red light on an empty road, when the sky is a pool of black"

i look at myself in the mirror and say, "you're allowed to be the death that comes a-knocking on doors,

and you are allowed to be unpredictable."

- you're allowed to be unpredictable

i hope angels watch me walk away and weep

since i've been through with useless grace for years now,

and "kindness" is not my middle name

- the angels and i do not get along

witching hour

myself and me and the moon makes three

                    unremarkble girl's lullaby

i am stuck in an hourglass,

and it was pleasant in here at first,

until sand started to cloud my vision,

and my mother had to pronounce me dead

i am stuck in an hourglass,

and no one can hear me screaming—

these see-through walls are soundproof, anyway,

and my lungs are drowning in dry

i am stuck in an hourglass,

and now there is sand cemented to my skin,

sand matted into the locks of my hair,

sand forever-trapped in the spaces between my toes,

and i just had to watch you force yourself to forget me,

and fall in love with someone else

i am stuck in an hourglass,

and someone keeps flipping my new home over each
time i'm seconds away from suffocating

the first time it happened, i fell sick with vertigo,

but now, i grow tired of feeling anything at all

i am stuck in an hourglass:

an eternal lesson in the dangers of patience—

and a perfect hell created

specifically for me

- i am stuck in an hourglass (and there's nothing waiting
for me if i escape)

with the heart that was made of amethyst/i took in breath
when my intuition told me to/i only touched the pennies i
found if they were heads-up/and i skipped over cracks in
the sidewalk/with the gusto of a kindergartener/with the
heart that was made of amethyst/i saw through you right
away/but i ignored what *i knew* i knew/and the amethyst
cracked/and the amethyst *splintered*

- *with the heart that was made of amethyst*

oh, to be pandora/the sweet-faced, curious girl/who lived
in a perfect world/and simply asked for something better

- oh, to be pandora

if my body were a building/i suppose it'd be a lighthouse/a beacon of the desire to belong/amidst the void between bleak waves/it would spill light onto the night sky/across the sea/and into the eyes/of those wistful enough to notice it/it would house climbing moss/and resilient wildflowers/walls, half-waterlogged/and broken pieces of beer bottles/if my body were a building/nature would fight to take it back/with its raging/beating/watery hands/and i/would simply let it

- if my body were a building

in another life, i was a goddess/who didn't love a thing/i had igniter fluid for blood/and i sang, shamelessly/for a spark

- spark

she has cheeks made out of rosebuds

that bloom bright crimson at any small delight,

but for fingernails, she has black thorns,

as she's been hurt too many times

to be foolish enough to decide

against growing herself protection

- a delicate destroyer

i sit with athena on thursdays,

and she laughs at my taste in books;

the weathered, browning pages amuse her to no end,

since she can't believe that even paper was given the
opportunity to age

before a *goddess*

got the glorious chance

whenever i thumb through one of their pages,

gaze half on the wall,

with a roll of her all-knowing eyes,

she takes the old thing out of my hands,

and replaces it with her fingers

we sit outside together at nighttime

with the expanse of a grey, cloudy sky above our heads

the light rain washes away our shared exhaustion,

as well as our superiority complexes

i sit with athena on thursdays,

and though she laughs at my taste in books,

she smiles at me when she thinks i'm not looking,

tells me to listen to whatever the thunder has to say when
it booms,

and ensures i let my inhibitions

crack and break with lightning bolts

- i sit with athena on thursdays

i don't want to dance amongst the stars—

i want to drown in them,

and be welcomed by near-immortal bodies, made of oblivion,

who see their likeness in me

                                        - brethren

your love is as sticky as spiderwebs,

and what an honor it is

to be caught in your snare

- son of arachne

the sight of your midnight fingers/drawing sigils into my moon-kissed skin/is something i simply shouldn't regard/as raptly as i do/i guess it's a bit like the fascination/that comes with watching planes crash/or, better yet, the *wonderment*/that walks hand-in-hand/with watching gods/as they shed their human vessels/to sear the eyes of awestruck mortals/with the heat of their silver divinity

- the gods, plane crashes, and your midnight fingers

delilah hands me a pair of scissors,

and tells me to cut your hair

she wants me to see what men are made of

once you take their strength away

   - delilah and i owe samson and you nothing

in a gilded cage lays a tortured muse,

who has been taught to take pleasure in the music

that he-who-keeps-the-key composes in her image

and though she used to rattle her prison's bars with clenched fists,

and though she used to plaster her palms to her ears to keep any hints of his siren songs at bay,

now, she hums along to the tune of her own petrification—

drunk off the idea

of being remembered

- muse

i prayed upon the purple lightning

that reared against the tossing waves of a dark sea

it saw me on my knees,

and in turn, made a pass at me,

littering my skin in bruises made of galaxy flecks—

now badges of a violent love

that i wear with the cooked heart on my sleeve

*- from the point of view of one of zeus's many mortal
lovers*

i dream of you and i, in space/strolling along the sky's endless perimeter like we own the place/i dream of you putting a star in my hair/the same way you did with the baby's breath that you plucked from the side of the road/the summer we drove through towns/that were just as indistinguishable as we were(/since no one could tell where one's borders ended/and where the other's began)/i dream of watching the end of the world with you/bearing witness as our childhood home/burns to nada-nilch-nothing/the second its star explodes/and i dream of smiling at the sight/safe/in our canopy of black clouds/and doted on/by our adoptive suns

- i dream of you and i, in space

because heaven will not grant me wings/i will fashion a pair for myself out of hot glue/and the forgotten, shed feathers of birds who have long-outgrown them/i will take leave of the earth at high noon/and to die/by plummeting into the crystalline water beneath me/after flying too close to the sun/would be a privilege/not condemnation/an *honor*/not karma

- a word or two in regards to icarus

i didn't mean to learn from sirens,

but they taught me something new:

"coat the skin of your pain in the scent of sweet nothings,

and just *watch* how quickly those around you succumb"

- school lessons from sirens

i thought it would be whimsy to put a funhouse mirror in
my bedroom,

but the mirage that greeted me there had bloodshot eyes,

and wore a cheshire cat grin

"who are you?" i asked, and she chuckled at my naïveté

"oh, sweet girl," she simpered,

"i'm the one who could do your life

a little better than you could."

- a challenger

i wish i were the waves that the moon commands

so i could feel nothing as i lay waste to the lives of my
admirers

i wish i were the waves that the moon commands

so i could be there to witness sea water

fill my poor, defenseless lungs

- i wish i were the waves that the moon commands

this is ~~a message~~ an ode to venus:

leave me alone

you disguise love in frills and powder,

in the whipped cream on milkshakes, and the red cherry on top

you watch with a smirk as i start to crave after it,

as i start to *wish upon numbers for it,*

and then,

you use my heart as your sacred war grounds,

and those who trod upon its strings

dirty it with loveless grime and murderous passion

they leave with my blood splattered red across their chests,

the shards of my heart they collected now spoils of a never-ending fight.

tell me, venus, is it you who likes the gore,

or mars?

or both?

perhaps that's why when the damage is done,

my heart heals itself with the gift of your ichor,

and the battle wages on

- an ode to venus

hello?/yes, i'm sitting at the bottom of a wishing well/i
have a broken arm/and the coin i threw/stubbornly
clasped in the other, very bruised fist/you see, i knew i
had to jump in after it/not because i needed the
money/but because i realized how ridiculous it would
be/to waste my precious pennies on him, too/on top of
everything else

- a 911 call from a wishing well

i'd like to give medusa a haircut,

then stick the shorn strands of her snakes onto my own scalp with tape

and even though the once-green serpents would have long since turned grey,

i've just wanted to *feel* what it is to be powerful enough

to *stop people before they can get to you*

- i'd like to give medusa a haircut

did you feel that the *blessing*

of that swirling, shining sky

was just a worthless product

of another spell-less, stuffy night?

if you did, be grateful,

for i envy your view—

i envy your *eternity*,

and i'd like to switch with you

- for the inhabitants of van gogh's imaginary village in
"the starry night"

there is something divinely comforting

in the idea that gods can die—

that to the universe, these luminescent beings

are just as fleeting as the humans/ants they step on

- forever in the blink of an eye

six fifty-eight

iamtiredofwastingtimeiamtiredofwastingtimeIAMTIRED
OFWASTINGTIME—

i blink at the intruding light that finds my eyes/despite the blankets and the tangled curls and the day-old clothes/of which i've made my armor out of/i blink until i get bored/i blink/until i wonder how long i have to/i blink/until daytime's brilliance shaves away my peach fuzz to make me look presentable/i blink/until it turns its attention to my sternum/and scorches apart the skin/that once protected my chest/i blink/until it emancipates my heart from its (rib) cage/the part of me that my foresight tried, in vain/to lock away

- jail break

there's no use in standing still—

i've started to grow roots

*- and everyone knows that roots are nature's very own
version of prison shackles*

the sun is done with seeing my tears,

so with his rays,

he dries them for me

he loves me too much to see me drown myself in self-
pity,

so he shines through my curtains to make me wake,

allows flowers to bloom like breakthroughs to goad me to
smell them,

and paints the evening sky in salmon and cerulean,

in violet and verdigris—

a colorfully stark reminder

that life can be so much more

than just about me.

- other father

darling little golden boy,

you've officially lost your shine

tell me, how did it feel to be outed as plastic

once your glimmer wore away?

- darling little golden boy, revisited

the world is my oyster,

and i'll shuck it open with my canines

- and may my teeth come back unbloodied

i will no longer spend my days staring at walls,

placated in their whispered falsehoods that patience would reward me

i will spend the rest of my life *punching* down those walls

until my knuckles come back split open

until my lungs hurt from breathing so hard

until i've never felt more *alive*

until i've never been more willing to die

- out

young woman, remember:

you change the future as you move.

- you are time

this little life i've made for myself

might not even make it to the footnotes of history books

but i am worth *at least* a paragraph—

no, *we* are worth *collections*

- let's find glory together

about the author

zhara eri's real name isn't actually "zhara eri"/she just thought it sounded cooler than her god-given/hallelujah/amen name/there's not much to analyze on that front/unlike everything else

Instagram: @zharaeripoetry

i hope the fly on my wall

enjoyed the scene that it just saw:

in it, a girl tore the heart out of her chest,

and sent it away for publishing

- fin

Readers agree that unremarkable girl's lullaby *is "a raw and honest story of life, love, and heartbreak":*

"Zhara Eri's debut poetry collection, *unremarkable girl's lullaby*, is breathtaking. She pulls her readers into the depths of her mind, and you will quickly find yourself lost among her beautiful expressions of emotion. Reading this book allows for the incredible experience of watching as her love turns from a new flame, to a raging fire, to something cold, icing over her heart and turning it bitter with time. However, what is even more incredible, is watching as she reclaims her power. This book tells a vivid story of the journey from love, to heartache, to something even more than healing. A fire clearly builds in the author's heart as she learns to find love within herself, instead of at the hands of someone else. I was genuinely unable to put this down once I started reading it—I just couldn't wait to see what absolutely inspired image Zhara would create next. I finished this book with a feeling of hope, peace, and empowerment—and I know anyone else who reads it will as well."

— *Maddie McGlinchey, author of,* "you're still in my passenger seat"…and other ghost stories*, admin of* @mgm.poetry

"A collection of literary works like no other: a riveting, emotional, and sometimes even heartbreaking journey through the starry abyss of an ironically remarkable girl's mind. The perfectly imperfect pictures that Zhara puts into her readers' brains with the intensity of her descriptive words form an entire constellation of profound feelings."

— Scott Spencer, admin of @lakeoflyrics

"Beautifully real; feels like drifting through a dream."

— Mal, admin of @mal_does_poetry

"Filled to the brim with melodic, flowing vocabulary, and heart-wrenchingly honest emotions."

— Megan, admin of @apatheticroommate

ISBN: 9798565479393